ro   y

Ian Graham

Evans

Published by Evans Brothers Limited

© 2011 Evans Brothers Ltd

Evans Brothers Limited
2A Portman Mansions
Chiltern Street
London W1U 6NR

First published 2011

British Library Cataloguing in Publication Data
Graham, Ian.
  Robot technology. -- (New technology)
  1. Robotics--Juvenile literature.
  I. Title II. Series
  629.8'92-dc22

  ISBN-13: 978 0 2375 4075 3

Printed by New Era Printing Co. Ltd, China

Credits

Series Editor: Paul Humphrey
Editor: Kathryn Walker
Designer: sprout.uk.com
Illustrations: Stefan Chabluk
Production: Jenny Mulvanny
Picture researcher: Kathryn Walker

Acknowledgements

Cover, title page and p41 TOPIO (www.topio.tosy.com); p6 Kim Jae-Hwan/ AFP/Getty Images; p7 Kazuhiro Nogi/ AFP/Getty Images; p8, 9, 10, 11, 12 NASA/ courtesy of nasaimages.org; p13 (top) NASA; p13 (bottom) NASA/Jet Propulsion Laboratory; p14 NASA; p15 ©2002, Georgia Institute of Technology/Georgia Tech Research Institute; p16 Aladin Abdel Naby/Reuters/CORBIS; p18 Reuters/ Royal New Zealand Navy/Handout/ Corbis; p17 NASA/Carnegie Mellon University/Science Photo Library; p20 Stone Aerospace/PSC, Inc./Bill Stone; p21 Photo by Rob Felt, ©2008 Georgia Institute of Technology/Georgia Tech Research Institute; p22 QinetiQ; p23 Carnegie Mellon University; p24 US Air Force photo/ Lt Col Leslie Pratt; p25 DARPA; p26 US Marine Corps photo by Lance Cpl ML Meier; p27 Wikimedia Commons (Toshinori Baba); p28 Gideon Mendel/Corbis; p30 iRobot Corp; p31 Toru Yamanaka/AFP/ Getty Images; pp32 and 33 ©InTouch Health; pp34 and 35 © 2009 Intuitive Surgical, Inc; p36 Kadak/Shutterstock.com; p37 Koichi Kamoshida/Getty Images; p38 Yoshikazu Tsuno/AFP/Getty Images; p39 Massimo Brega, The Lighthouse/Science Photo Library; p40 Malte Christians/Bongarts/ Getty Images; p42 Yoshikazu Tsuno/AFP/ Getty Images; p43 SM/AIUEO/Stone/ Getty Images.

This book was prepared for Evans Brothers by Discovery Books Ltd. (www.discoverybooks.net)

contents

introduction

A robot is a machine, either automatic or remotely controlled, that can do some of the things people can do. There are about 6.5 million robots in use in the world today. A million of them are industrial robots, building cars and other products in factories. Most of the other 5.5 million are service robots, working in hospitals, offices and homes. The remaining 55,000 robots work on land, under the sea, in the air and in space.

Smart machines More and more robots are working in industry, but there are very few robots in people's homes and none walking about outdoors. Walking, talking robots, looking and behaving just like people often appear in science-fiction movies, but in reality these robots do not exist yet. It is very difficult to get robots to do some of the things that people find easy – walking, running, jumping, understanding speech and recognising complicated shapes and patterns. The computers that control robots cannot yet match the power of a human brain, but they're getting faster and more powerful all the time. As a result, robots are getting smarter too.

Some robots have mechanical hands that look like, and work like, human hands.

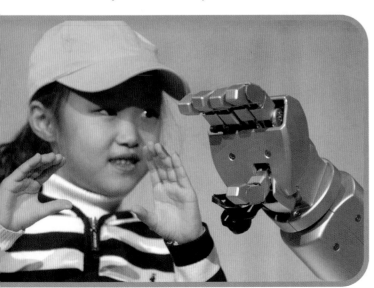

BIRTH OF THE ROBOT

The word 'robot' was invented in the early 1900s by Josef Capek. His brother, the Czech playwright Carel Capek, had written a play about a factory where artificial humans work. While looking for a name for the mechanical workers, Josef suggested the name robota. It means hard work, especially forced work or slave labour. The play, which was published in 1920, was called *Rossum's Universal Robots.*

PaPeRo is a Japanese robot that can recognise people's faces, understand what is said to it and speak back.

Senses Humans have five senses: touch, taste, sight, hearing and smell. The most advanced robots have at least two senses – sight and touch – so that they can see the world around them

WHAT'S NEXT?

The robot population is growing fast. By 2012, the number of robots in use worldwide is expected to rise to more than 18 million. South Korea aims to put a robot in every home there by 2020 at the latest. By then, nearly a third of the US Army may be staffed by robots, from self-driving vehicles and flying spies to fighting robots. By 2050, there may be more robots in the world than there are cars today.

and know when they have bumped into something. They see by using cameras for eyes. Cameras record images, but they can't understand what the images mean. For this, a robot needs computer programs to analyse what its camera-eyes see. Some robots are able to hear by using microphones as ears. Robots can also have extra senses that people don't have. A robot with infrared (heat-sensing) cameras can see in the dark.

Although robots can't do some of the things that are simple to us, they can do other things far better than we can. They have better memories than humans – robots don't forget. Robots don't get tired and some are far stronger than the strongest human.

CHAPTER 1
space robots

Robots are already working in space. The Space Shuttle and International Space Station (ISS) have robot arms and robot rovers are exploring Mars. Robot spacecraft are flying to remote parts of the solar system. Meanwhile, new robots are being designed for future manned and unmanned space missions.

Robot arms The Space Shuttle is a spacecraft that visits the ISS in orbit periodically. Both spacecraft have robot arms that can pick up and move massive loads. The arms manoeuvre new parts of the ISS into position. The Space Shuttle's robot arm is 15 metres long and it can handle objects that weigh more than 29 tonnes on Earth. The space station's arm is a little longer,

Two astronauts at the end of the Space Shuttle's robot arm carry out repairs to the Hubble Space Telescope.

HOW IT WORKS

The robot arms on board the Space Shuttle and International Space Station are controlled by a computer. The computer operates motorised joints in the arms. When an astronaut operates a control to move the arm, the computer moves the joints so that the arm does what the astronaut wants it to do. Cameras on the arms show the astronaut what the arm is doing.

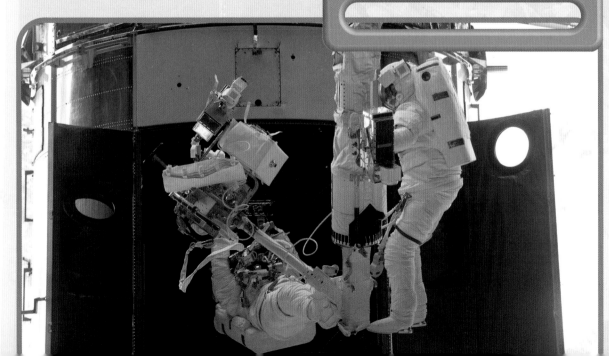

17 metres, and can handle much larger loads up to 116 tonnes. One end of the Shuttle's robot arm is fixed to the spacecraft's payload bay (cargo-carrying space), but the space station's arm is not fixed in one place. It can move itself around to reach different parts of the space station. The arms are operated by astronauts inside the spacecraft.

Robots on Mars The Spirit and Opportunity rovers landed on Mars in January, 2004. Both run on six wheels. Power for the wheels and instruments is supplied by solar panels that change sunlight into electricity. The rovers were designed to explore the ground around their landing sites for 90 days, but were still working years later.

An artist's view of one of the twin Mars rovers as it explores the surface of the planet, guided by its own navigation system.

HOW IT WORKS

Controllers on Earth tell Spirit and Opportunity where they want the rovers to go next. Then each rover looks ahead with its cameras and makes a 3D map of the ground. Using this map, the rover plans the safest route to its destination, avoiding rocks and other dangers on the way. It must avoid toppling over because it would be unable to turn itself upright again.

Spirit and Opportunity are controlled from Earth. They can't be driven like radio-controlled cars, because a radio signal takes several minutes to reach Mars. Instead, they have enough intelligence to steer themselves to the places controllers are most interested in.

Space probes Spacecraft that fly to the furthest regions of the solar system go so far from Earth that they have to be able to look after themselves if anything goes wrong. The latest interplanetary probes don't have to wait for controllers on Earth to decide on everything for them.

The New Horizons space probe is on its way to the tiny, frozen world, Pluto. It was launched in 2006, but Pluto is so far away that it will not

HOW IT WORKS

The New Horizons space probe needs to know which way it is facing, so that its instruments and radio aerials point in the right direction. Ten times a second, a camera on the probe takes a picture of space and compares it to a map of 3,000 stars in its memory. If the spacecraft decides that it is facing the wrong way, it fires small rockets or gas jets known as thrusters to correct its position.

arrive until 2015. New Horizons is programmed to check its own systems, look for faults and, if it finds any, fix them. If it tries everything but still can't fix a problem, it phones home. The space probe sends a message to Earth asking for help. Then the mission controllers on Earth can try things that the probe isn't programmed to do itself. For example, they can fire its thrusters to shake a sticking antenna free or they can send up new software to change the way the probe operates to work round a defective part.

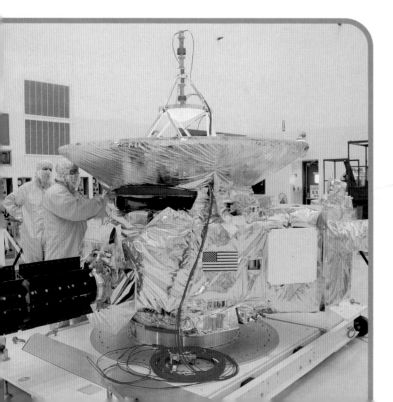

Engineers put the finishing touches to the New Horizons space probe. The engineers' clothing stops hair, skin flakes or fingerprints getting onto the probe and perhaps causing a fault.

NUCLEAR POWER

Unmanned spacecraft are usually powered by electric current made from sunlight by solar panels. Space probes that visit the furthest planets go too far from the Sun to make electricity from sunlight. Instead, they are nuclear powered. The New Horizons Pluto probe has a nuclear electricity generator. The plutonium fuel it contains stays hot because it is radioactive. This heat is converted into electricity.

Robot astronauts The US space agency NASA has developed a robot astronaut, called Robonaut, to do some of the work outside a spacecraft that usually has to be done today by spacewalking astronauts. Robonaut looks like a human astronaut's head, body, arms and hands. Its fingers move like human fingers. Robonaut is controlled by an astronaut inside the spacecraft. The astronaut wears a head-mounted screen and sees whatever the robot is looking at. When the astronaut moves his or her hands and arms, the robot's hands and arms move in the same way. NASA launched the first Robonaut into space in February 2011. It became a permanent resident of the International Space Station.

Robot scouts NASA has developed robots that astronauts can use to explore the surface of a planet such as the Moon or Mars. One of these robots is a small rover vehicle called K10 that could be sent out to survey the land around a new moonbase or the astronauts' landing craft. Moving at human walking speeds, K10 can measure the height and slope

NASA's Robonaut (below) is a robot designed to help humans work and explore in space.

of the terrain with radar to see what lies beneath it. Radar detects layers of soil and rock under the ground by sending out radio waves and receiving any reflections that bounce back from them. Getting robots to do this could save hundreds of hours of walks by astronauts.

FOR AND AGAINST

Is it better to use robot astronauts instead of humans?

For
- Robot astronauts save humans from the dangers of spacewalks.
- They can work for far longer than a spacewalking astronaut.
- Robots are expendable, astronauts are not.
- Robots in space do not need food, water or air.

Against
- Space robots are more limited than humans in what they can physically do and need human guidance.
- They move more slowly than human astronauts.
- If they malfunction, space robots can become space junk and a danger to spacecraft.
- Humans can solve problems without guidance and respond quickly to unexpected situations. Robots cannot.

K10 is the prototype of a small robot for making detailed maps of the ground.

Moonbase When the Apollo astronauts went to the Moon in the 1960s and 1970s, they lived in their spacecraft, the Lunar Excursion Module. The equipment they had to move around was light enough to carry. If astronauts go back to the Moon, they might set up a moonbase to live in. For this to happen, they would need to move tonnes of equipment. The astronauts couldn't possibly carry all of it themselves, but NASA has been developing a cargo-carrying robot called ATHLETE that would help them. ATHLETE stands for All-Terrain Hex-Legged Extra-Terrestrial Explorer. It can roll along on the wheels at the end of its six legs, or it can lock the wheels and walk like a giant insect.

WHAT'S NEXT?

Future cargo robots and robot astronauts will understand voice commands and hand gestures so that astronauts will be able to control them more easily and more naturally. Some robots can already understand a little human speech. Others understand a few hand gestures. The challenge is to improve these abilities and build them into intelligent space robots that will work reliably and safely.

This is an artist's idea of what a moonbase of the future might look like.

ATHLETE can move at 10 kph across the same sort of ground that the Apollo astronauts landed on – that's 100 times faster than the Mars rovers, Spirit and Opportunity. It can also climb slopes of rock or loose sand. Each ATHLETE can carry up to

450 kg of cargo. Two or more can be linked together to carry heavier loads. Prototypes of the small surveying rover and the ATHLETE cargo-carrying rover have already been tested on Earth.

These two ATHLETE rovers are being tested in the California desert. They are six-legged robots that could help astronauts set up a base on the Moon.

An artist's impression of a robot plane flying above the surface of Mars. In future, planes like this may be sent to explore the planet from a height of only 1.5 km.

Scarab If astronauts go back to the Moon, they would probably stay there for several weeks or months at a time. They couldn't take everything they would need, so they would have to extract some essential elements from the lunar rocks and soil. A little robot called Scarab is being developed for testing lunar soil for substances that astronauts could extract and use, such as hydrogen, oxygen and water.

Flying on Mars The planet Mars has an atmosphere, which robot aircraft could fly through. A flying robot could explore a much bigger area than a rover on the ground. It could also take more detailed pictures and measurements than a satellite in orbit. Prototypes of new flying robots for exploring Mars are being tested now.

Three types of flying robots could be sent to Mars. The simplest is a balloon that drifts with the wind. The second is an airship. It would float in the atmosphere like a balloon, but, powered by a propeller, it would be able to steer itself in any direction. The third type of flying robot is a plane – either a glider or a propeller-driven plane.

Take-off NASA has decades of experience putting space probes into orbit around Mars and landing craft on the surface, but so far no-one has put a flying robot on Mars. It would be difficult to get a robot plane off the ground. The thicker the air, the more lift a wing generates at a particular speed. The Martian atmosphere is thinner than Earth's. Therefore, a Martian plane would need very big wings or a very fast take-off run to produce enough lift from the thin atmosphere to get airborne. And of course there are no long, smooth runways on Mars. Instead, a robot plane will probably be launched as it enters the atmosphere from space.

The plane will enter the Martian atmosphere folded up inside a shell. The shell will protect it from the heat caused by plunging into the atmosphere at great speed. As it hurtles towards the ground, a parachute will slow it down. Then the shell will pop open and the plane will unfold and fly away. Models of the Mars plane have been tested in wind tunnels and flown in the Earth's atmosphere at an altitude of 31,500 metres.

Flapping wings Scientists at Georgia Tech Research Institute in the USA have been working on a different sort of flying robot for Mars. Called an entomopter, it looks like a big insect with flapping wings. It would travel on the back of a rover and fly off to investigate interesting features spotted by the rover's cameras. The scientists have already developed an artificial muscle to flap the wings.

WHAT'S NEXT?

Tiny hopping robots called frogbots may be sent to explore other worlds. A swarm of 1,000 frogbots, each about the size of a tennis ball, could cover far more ground than one rover vehicle. They can also hop around on rough, rocky ground where wheeled rovers would get stuck. Solar cells, making electricity from sunlight, could recharge the robot's batteries between jumps. Hopping space robots are being developed now in the USA and Switzerland.

This is a model of the flying insect explorer robot, or entomopter. It is being developed for surveillance and data collection on Mars.

CHAPTER 2
earth explorers

Robots explore places that are too dangerous or difficult for people to explore, such as active volcanoes, narrow underground passageways or deep underwater. Most robot explorers are remotely controlled by an operator, but some are able to make their own decisions about where to go and how to get there.

Pyramid Rover In 2002, a miniature robot called the Pyramid Rover, just 12 cm wide, was inserted into a narrow tunnel in the heart of Egypt's Great Pyramid. Archaeologists wanted to know where the tunnel went and what it contained. Lights and a camera on the front of the rover showed its operators what lay ahead of it.

The rover crawled up the tunnel for 65 metres and then came up to a stone door. It drilled a hole through the door and inserted a camera, but the view

The Pyramid Rover is a robot specially designed to explore a mysterious tunnel in an Egyptian pyramid.

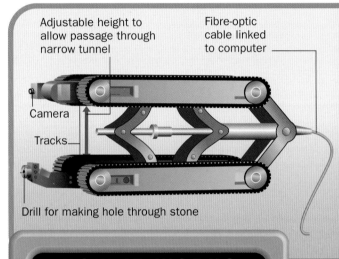

Adjustable height to allow passage through narrow tunnel

Fibre-optic cable linked to computer

Camera

Tracks

Drill for making hole through stone

HOW IT WORKS

The Pyramid Rover had to climb up a steeply inclined, narrow tunnel. To give it maximum grip, it ran on tracks, like tank tracks. The rover had tracks on top as well as underneath. They pushed against the ceiling and floor of the tunnel, wedging the rover in position and stopping it from sliding backwards. The rover was operated by means of a control box connected to the rover by cable.

ahead was blocked by yet another door further on. No-one had seen this second door since the pyramid builders put it there 4,000 years earlier.

Walking into volcanoes Scientists studying volcanoes and their effect on the atmosphere would like to take samples of gas from inside their craters. However, the crater of an active volcano is one of the most dangerous places on Earth.

In the 1990s, scientists at Carnegie Mellon University in Pennsylvania, USA, built a robot called Dante for exploring volcano craters. It was an eight-legged walking robot. As it explored the crater of Mount Erebus in Antarctica, its communications cable broke. It then had to be winched out of the crater. The robot was rebuilt as Dante II, which successfully descended into the crater of Mount Spurr in Alaska, USA in 1994.

NASA paid for the Dante robots, because lessons learned from building and operating them help scientists to design walking robots that will be sent to the Moon and planets in future. While wheeled robots like Spirit and Opportunity are good for exploring reasonably level ground, walking robots are better suited to going up and down steep slopes and climbing over boulders.

The Dante II robot begins its exploration of the crater of Mount Spurr, an active volcano in Alaska. NASA may use similar robots in the future to explore the surface of the Moon or planets.

Deep divers The deepest parts of the world's oceans are the most difficult to explore. The Challenger Deep in the Marianas Trench, near the island of Guam in the western Pacific Ocean, is the deepest of all. The bottom is 11,000 metres below the ocean surface – as deep below the surface as an airliner flies above it. The water pressure there is a crushing 1,000 times the surface pressure. Most of the deep-diving robots that explore the oceans can reach a depth of 6,500 metres at most. Only three vehicles have ever visited the Challenger Deep. A manned craft called Trieste touched down in 1960 and a Japanese robot called Kaiko made it in 1995 and 1998. The third was a robot called Nereus, in 2009.

Dual purpose Robot divers like Kaiko are linked to a mother-ship by a cable. A pilot in the ship steers the vehicle. Robots that work in this way are known as remotely operated vehicles (ROVs). The deepest diving vehicle today is Nereus. It can be used in two

ways. It can work like a normal diving robot, controlled by an operator in a ship connected to Nereus by a cable. It can also have its cable disconnected and work as a free-swimming vehicle controlling itself.

First, Nereus is sent into the depths as a free-swimming autonomous robot, to map the ocean floor. Scientists look at the maps and spot the most interesting places. Then Nereus is sent down again as a remotely operated vehicle. The pilot steers it towards the most interesting targets for a closer look. Live pictures are sent up from its cameras along a fibre-optic cable. Nereus also has a mechanical arm for collecting samples of ocean floor sediments and small creatures.

This image of a sunken ferry on the Pacific Ocean floor was taken from an ROV in 2009.

ROVs

Remotely Operated Vehicles (ROVs) were invented in the 1950s to find practice torpedoes fired by submarines. Since then, ROVs have found all sorts of lost objects, including sunken ships and even a hydrogen bomb dropped in the Mediterranean Sea by an aircraft. Today, as well as undersea exploration, they are used to inspect underwater structures. These include pipelines, communications cables and the legs of oil and gas drilling platforms.

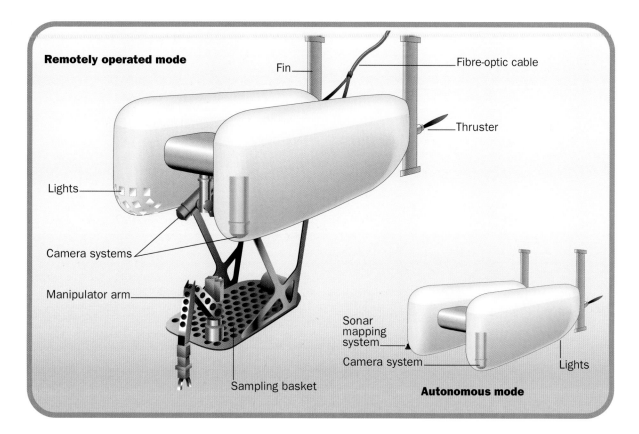

Remotely operated mode

Fin

Fibre-optic cable

Thruster

Lights

Camera systems

Manipulator arm

Sampling basket

Sonar mapping system

Camera system

Lights

Autonomous mode

Nereus is a unique diving robot designed to explore the deepest parts of the world's oceans. It can be remotely operated but can also work as a free-swimming vehicle.

Autonomous subs Fully autonomous diving robots are programmed for each mission, which they carry out on their own without any human contact or control. Robots that do this are known as autonomous underwater vehicles (AUVs). Some of them stay at sea for days or weeks, making maps and collecting information. These robots are helping scientists to understand the geological, chemical and biological processes that occur deep underwater.

HOW IT WORKS

Electrically-powered propellers called thrusters propel a diving robot through the water and also steer it. The thruster motors are powered by the robot's batteries. There are several thrusters. Each thruster is usually fixed in one position and does not swivel. The thrusters are fitted to the robot so that they point in different directions. By choosing which thruster or thrusters to use, the robot can move or turn in any direction.

Diving saucers DEPTHX is a saucer-shaped robot built in 2006. It looks like an alien spaceship and it does have a link with spaceflight. NASA was involved with DEPTHX, because one day they plan to send autonomous robots like DEPTHX to explore seas on distant moons.

DEPTHX makes maps of underwater caves and flooded mines. In 2007 it mapped the world's deepest water-filled hole, a sink-hole in Mexico. This is a hole in the ground big enough to swallow a skyscraper. DEPTHX dived into it and made a map of the shape of the walls. It also stretched out an arm and took samples from the walls.

The DEPTHX robot has been redesigned to make it suitable for exploring ice-covered waters. This new version is called ENDURANCE. In 2008 and 2009 it explored and mapped the waters of Lake Bonney, a permanently ice-covered lake in Antarctica.

The ENDURANCE AUV undergoes testing in Wisconsin, USA. NASA may one day use robot explorers like this to dive into a sea on Jupiter's moon, Europa.

HOW IT WORKS

Underwater robots use sonar to make maps of the ocean floor. Sonar (SOund Navigation and Ranging) works by sending pulses of sound down through the water and detecting any reflections, or echoes, that bounce back. The time an echo takes to arrive tells the robot exactly how far away the ocean floor is.

Gliders While some diving robots map the seabed, others study the ocean itself. They measure its temperature, salinity (saltiness) and other ocean properties. Some of these robots are vehicles called gliders. They have wings like gliding aircraft, but they glide through water instead of air.

A deep-diving glider called Seaglider sinks to a depth of 1,000 metres, taking measurements on the way, and then rises again to the surface. When it surfaces, it reports back to base automatically by using its own satellite phone.

Seaglider can travel at steep angles. This allows the robot to return to the surface close to the spot where it entered the water.

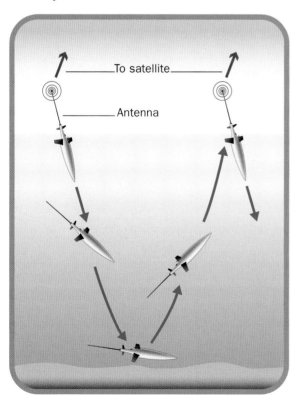

A scientist works on a SnoMote. This is a robot designed for gathering data in polar regions.

WHAT'S NEXT?

Future exploration of the Earth's polar regions may be done by robots called SnoMotes. Robots that travel over the ice can make more accurate measurements than satellites, although satellites can monitor larger areas. The development of the SnoMotes is being funded by NASA. The information SnoMotes collect will help scientists to understand how climate change is affecting the vast ice sheets that surround the Earth's poles.

CHAPTER 3
military machines

Thousands of robots are in military service. Most of them are designed to spy on an enemy, probe the land ahead of advancing troops for hidden dangers and search caves and buildings. Far more advanced military robots than these are already being designed and built.

Remote control The most numerous military robots are small, remote-control vehicles like Talon. A soldier drives it by using a remote control linked to the robot by cable or by radio. Talon is fast. It can easily keep up with a running soldier. The control unit has a screen that shows a picture from the robot's colour or infrared cameras. Infrared cameras make pictures from heat instead of light, so they are especially useful in the dark.

Robots like Talon can be fitted with a variety of tools, including a gripper (a mechanical hand), a wire cutter and a shotgun.

HOW IT WORKS

Small military robots often run on tracks, like tanks. The tracks are rubber belts that fit over the wheels. Tracks give a robot more grip on loose surfaces and soft ground. They make steering simple, too. The tracks don't have to turn in order to steer the robot. Slowing or stopping the track on one side makes the robot turn in that direction.

The shotgun is used to destroy enemy booby traps and to blow the locks off doors. Some of the robots have sensors that detect dangerous chemicals or explosives.

US military forces have over 2,000 Talon robots, more than any other kind of military robot. The Talon robot in this picture is being used for detecting and clearing mines.

Tough cookies Military robots have to be very rugged machines. A Talon robot once fell off a vehicle as it drove across a bridge in Iraq and sank to the bottom of the river. Its operator was able to simply drive the robot out of the river. Talons have been used to deal with unexploded grenades and booby-trap bombs without putting soldiers at risk.

Armed robots It's a short step from fitting robots with guns for bomb disposal work to arming them for combat. The US Army has been testing armed robots since 2007. The SWORDS robot is a modified Talon, armed with a rifle, machine-gun or grenade launcher. Several teams of robot engineers are working on new combat robots. These include the Gladiator robot being developed for the US Marine Corps. It is the size of a small car with a machine-gun mounted on top.

Flying spies While robots like Talon crawl around on the ground, there are more robots in the air watching the ground. Some of them are unmanned spy-planes. Others are

WHAT'S NEXT?

The first combat robots will not fire their weapons unless the soldiers controlling them give the go-ahead, but later combat robots will probably be able to decide for themselves when to open fire. Before they are given the power to decide when to fire, they will have to be intelligent enough to tell the difference between friendly forces and the enemy by using advanced vision systems. This is very difficult – even soldiers sometimes get it wrong.

Future soldiers may go into combat alongside robots like this Gladiator.

WARRIOR

The iRobot Warrior 700 is a new military robot that can carry loads weighing up to 68 kg. It scoots along at 15 kph and can climb steps as well as travel over rough terrain. This powerful robot can be fitted with a robot arm or a machine-gun. The iRobot Warrior was designed to carry out tasks such as bomb disposal, route clearance, surveillance and moving casualties to safety.

deadly attack craft. Most of them are flown by pilots on the ground. Others fly themselves from take-off to landing. Without a pilot on board, flying robots can be smaller, lighter and simpler than manned aircraft and they can stay in the air for longer. Also, if an unmanned aircraft is lost or destroyed, no pilot's life is lost.

Unmanned Aerial Vehicles (UAVs)

The US Air Force's Predator is one of the most widely used robot planes. It looks like a small aircraft 8.2 metres long, with a wingspan of 14.8 metres. Ready for take-off, armed with two missiles, it weighs just over 1 tonne. A small engine spins a propeller at the back. The Reaper, another American robot aircraft, is bigger than Predator. It can fly higher and faster than Predator, stay in the air longer and carry more weapons.

Predator and Reaper are flown by a pilot sitting in a cockpit on the ground. The pilot looks at a screen showing the picture taken by a video camera in the plane's nose. The pilot and plane are in radio contact by satellite. When the pilot moves the flying controls, the plane climbs, dives or turns accordingly. It can circle over a target for hours waiting for the right moment to attack. It is so small and quiet and it flies so high that people on the ground may not know it is there until it fires its missiles.

Predator is a 'MALE' robot plane – Medium Altitude, Long Endurance.

Global Hawk The most advanced flying robots can carry out a mission, from take-off to landing, without any human control. Global Hawk is one of these autonomous planes. It is a jet-powered spy-plane the size of a small airliner. It cruises at 650 kph and flies as high as 20,000 metres. Global Hawk can circle a target on the ground for up to 24 hours and watch it with cameras, radar and infrared imagers. It might be looking for vehicles moving along a particular road or enemy forces gathering. A ground crew watches the plane's progress and can take over control if necessary.

The US Navy plans to station Unmanned Combat Air Vehicles (UCAVs), like this X-47, on their ships. This is an artist's impression of one landing on an aircraft carrier.

WHAT'S NEXT?

The opening shots in a future air war could be fought by robot planes called UCAVs (Unmanned Combat Air Vehicles). UCAVs are faster, more nimble and more deadly than robot aircraft like the Predator, which was designed as a spy-plane and then armed later. The UCAVs that are currently in development are designed to be autonomous, but a pilot on the ground could take control if necessary. The prototypes of some UCAVs are already flying today. Their job in a future war would be to destroy enemy air defences, such as radar installations and anti-aircraft missile bases, before manned fighters arrive.

FOR AND AGAINST

Is it better to use robot fighter-planes than fighters with pilots?

For
- Robot fighter-planes can perform more extreme manoeuvres, such as very tight turns, than fighters with pilots on board. If a pilot makes too tight a turn, he or she can lose consciousness.
- They save pilots from danger.

Against
- A faulty robot could attack the wrong target.
- Being able to attack without endangering pilots could make war more likely.

Two BigDog robots trot around while given commands by remote control.

Robot soldiers Soldiers have to carry more gear than ever before. Carrying a heavy backpack can slow down a soldier's reaction to an attack and risk the soldier's life. Robots are being developed to carry their gear instead. These robots cannot run on wheels or tracks, because they have to be able to go wherever a soldier goes on foot. They have to walk like a soldier. One of these walking robots is called BigDog. It's a four-legged robot about the size of a large dog or a small mule. It can carry a load of about 150 kg.

WHAT'S NEXT?

After four-legged robots like BigDog, the next step is to develop two-legged robot soldiers. One, called Petman, is already being built, but so far its only job is to test chemical protection clothing for the US Army. It will balance for itself, walk and crawl. It will also get hot and sweat like a real soldier, to test the clothing thoroughly in lifelike conditions. In future, a more advanced Petman could be walking alongside serving soldiers.

Robot sentries During a military operation, vehicles and buildings used by military forces have to be protected. This takes up a large number of soldiers. Some borders between countries have to be patrolled by troops too. Using robot guards instead of humans would free up these soldiers to do other things.

The first robot security guards are already at work. A Korean company has built an armed sentry robot for guarding borders. It is intelligent enough to tell whether it has an animal or a human in its gunsights. Unlike a human border guard, this robot can work 24 hours a day and it does not need to eat or sleep.

Centurion US military camps in high-risk areas overseas are protected by a robot gun called Centurion. It is a six-barrel gun that that can shoot down enemy rockets, artillery shells and mortars in mid-air. The gun fires up to 4,500 bullets per minute. The special bullets it uses are designed to self-destruct if they miss their target so that they don't injure anyone on the ground. There are not many of these robot guns in service yet, so soldiers still have to be prepared for enemy rocket, artillery and mortar attacks.

The Centurion robot gun can tilt and turn very quickly to aim its gun at incoming threats.

HOW IT WORKS

The Centurion robot gun uses radar to spot enemy rockets, shells and mortars as they fly through the air. Once the search radar spots a target, it hands over to the tracking radar, which locks onto the moving target. The radars are inside the tall casing on top of the gun. Then the gun fires and destroys the target.

CHAPTER 4
robot workers

Robots have been working in factories since 1961, when the first industrial robot, called Unimate, was installed at a General Motors car plant in the USA. Since then, robots have been installed in thousands of factories and warehouses all over the world. Now, robots are helping out at home too.

Robot arms Industrial robots in the shape of computer-controlled arms are a common sight in factories today. They cut materials, drill holes, weld metal parts together, paint products and move things from place to place. They have taken over a lot of the boring and repetitive jobs that people had to do in the past.

Some industrial robots are very strong. A robot the size of a person can easily lift a load of 50 kg, move it quickly and position it to within a fraction of a millimetre. The world's strongest industrial robot, the Kuka KR1000 Titan, can lift loads weighing up to a tonne.

Lines of robots build cars in a modern car factory.

The electronics industry uses robots to build circuit boards for all sorts of electronic products. These robots can pick up tiny electronic components one by one and place them on a circuit board with great accuracy. Robots that do this kind of work are called pick and place robots. They work faster and more accurately than a person doing the same job.

FOR AND AGAINST

For
- Robots don't need lunch breaks or holidays and they don't go on strike.
- They don't get tired or bored.
- They don't have to be paid wages.
- They work with great precision.
- They create new jobs at companies that make, service and repair robots.

Against
- Robots do work that used to be done by people, who will have to find work elsewhere.
- People have to learn new skills or need to retrain.
- Robots are not as versatile as people, because they can carry out only the tasks they are programmed for.
- They may not spot problems or faults they are not programmed to deal with.

HOW IT WORKS

An industrial robot's joints can be moved by high-pressure air or oil, but most robots are electric. Their muscle power is provided by electric motors. The motors give a big industrial robot as much power as a car. A robot arm with six motorised joints can move in the same way as a human arm. It is said to be a six-axis robot or to have six degrees of freedom.

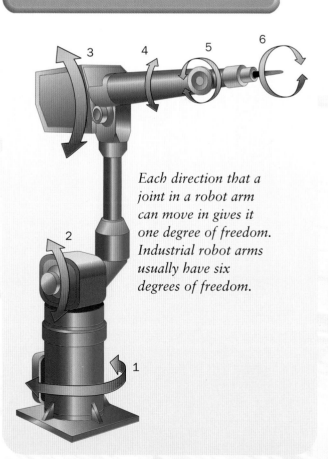

Each direction that a joint in a robot arm can move in gives it one degree of freedom. Industrial robot arms usually have six degrees of freedom.

Robots in the real world Robots in factories work with identical objects, such as car parts, positioned in exactly the same place every time. These robots follow the same series of operations over and over again. Robots that work in homes and offices have a more difficult task. They have to make sense of objects of all different shapes, sizes and colours. These robots need far more computing power to do their work.

Home and office Robots have become commonplace in industry, and now they are beginning to appear in public places. They are greeting customers in shops and doing simple fetch-and-carry jobs in offices, such as carrying files or delivering mail. There are robots to help out at home too. Robots that will vacuum carpets, wash floors or mow the grass are already on sale.

WHAT'S NEXT?

Future home service robots might include machines like uBot-5, a small experimental robot designed to help around the home. It can pick up things, carry them around and even phone for help in an emergency. A worried relative who can't get a response can access uBot-5 through the Internet and steer it around the home to check that everything is alright. The uBot-5 robot was built by researchers at the University of Massachusetts Amherst, USA.

Carry your bags? Travelling by air often involves carrying heavy suitcases long distances through airports. Baggage trolleys and suitcases with wheels make it a bit easier. RoboPorter makes it simple. As the name suggests, RoboPorter is a robot porter that can carry passengers' bags to a bus stop or taxi rank. It has been tested at Kitakyushu Airport in Japan. Passengers who want to use RoboPorter stand in front of it and tell it where they want to go. RoboPorter then carries the passengers' bags there.

This is iRobot's 'Scooba', a robot that navigates through rooms, cleaning, washing and drying floors as it goes.

Guide-bots A robot can store a building's floor layout in its memory, together with the locations of important items, such as paintings in an art gallery or exhibits in a museum. Add a computer-generated voice and you have a robot that can guide people around a building.

The Japanese company Fujitsu has produced a robot called Enon for guiding people. Enon can detect someone standing in front of it. A touch-sensitive screen in its chest shows information. Enon can talk and also produce facial expressions made from lights on its face. It can work in an office, carrying mail in a compartment in its body. Enon can also patrol a building as a security robot and transmit pictures wirelessly to a remote office.

Emergency robots Robots are also being built for emergency and rescue work. Robots called snakebots are especially useful. They look and move like a snake, enabling them to climb over things, swim in water and wriggle through tiny gaps. A Norwegian snakebot called Anna Konda is a firefighting robot. It has been designed to crawl into tight spaces or climb stairs and to direct a water spray onto a fire.

An Enon robot communicates with an engineer during a demonstration.

WHAT'S NEXT?

Snakebots will wriggle through the rubble of collapsed buildings after an earthquake searching for trapped victims. They could find survivors by homing in on their body heat or the carbon dioxide they breathe out. When they find survivors, the snakebots will carry water to them. Rescuers may be able to talk to trapped survivors via the snakebots.

CHAPTER 5
hospital bots

Three types of robots work in hospitals. One type carries files, meals, laboratory specimens and medical supplies around hospitals. The second type visits patients and lets a doctor hear, see and talk to them through the robot. The third type is the surgical robot, a robot that carries out surgery on patients.

Hospital helper HelpMate is a hospital porter robot. It has several lockable compartments for carrying things securely. As it travels along hospital corridors, a laser scanner detects obstacles, including people, and HelpMate automatically avoids them. It can even call a lift by radio to go to another floor. A study at one US hospital found that six HelpMate robots could replace 15 human porters. In this way, the robots would save enough money to pay for themselves in just over three years.

Doctor's rounds Robots like RP-7 enable a doctor to be in two places at once. The doctor can send the robot to a patient's bedside at a moment's notice. A camera in the robot's head lets the doctor see the patient, and the patient can see the doctor on the robot's screen. The doctor and patient can speak to each other through the robot too. Patients are often surprised to find themselves talking to their doctor via a robot, but it soon becomes as natural as talking to a doctor by telephone.

The RP-7 is a mobile robot that allows a doctor and patient to see and talk to each other when they are in different locations. The patient sees the doctor's face on a screen.

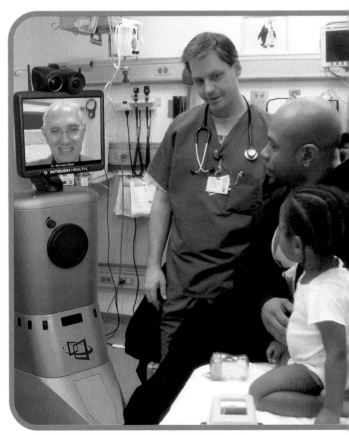

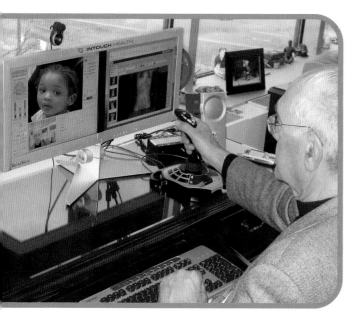

A doctor sits at a control station linked to the RP-7 by Internet and communicates with the patient pictured on page 32. The RP-7 also allows the doctor to talk with hospital staff.

FOR AND AGAINST

For
- Robot carers make up for shortages in hospital staff.
- Robots can be programmed to provide high-quality care for long periods.

Against
- Robots lack the personal touch of human carers.
- Some patients, especially those who are confused, could become frightened by the robots.

WHAT'S NEXT?

As populations age and more people need care, robots will take over more of the routine heavy lifting, transportation of mail, medicine, meals, files and so on in hospitals and care homes, freeing some of the staff for more important duties. It also means that fewer staff are likely to be employed. Force Technology in Sweden is developing a new generation of hospital robots for carrying materials around hospitals, with prototypes due to be tested in a Swedish hospital in 2011.

RP-7 can also connect to patient monitoring equipment and send data to the doctor about the patient's health. Robots like this enable doctors to check patients, even if the doctor is some distance away. More than 100 RP-7 robots are working in hospitals in the USA, Canada, UK, France, Italy and Turkey.

Surgical robots Robots are now being used in hospital operating theatres. They are not taking the place of surgeons, but enable surgeons to improve the quality of their work. Robots can move surgical instruments more steadily and more precisely than a surgeon's hands can manage. When the surgeon moves the controls, the robot doesn't just make the instruments copy his or her hand movements. It makes smaller, more precise movements and automatically removes any shaking in the surgeon's hands. The robots also make smaller incisions (cuts) in the patient's body and cause less bleeding and pain. As a result, patients recover from their operations more quickly.

Remote control Surgical robots have two main parts. The first is the control console where the surgeon sits and operates the robot. The second is the robot itself. It stands beside the patient and carries out the operation. The surgeon looks through a pair of eyepieces linked to cameras looking at the patient. The surgeon sees a

3D view of the operation. When the surgeon moves a pair of hand controllers, the robot's computer moves the instruments accordingly.

Doctor da Vinci One of the most famous and widely used surgical robots is the American da Vinci system. The da Vinci robot has up to four arms. They hold probes that go through tiny incisions in the patient's skin and hold instruments inside the patient. Various cutting and gripping tools can be fitted to the robot's arms. The first two arms act like the surgeon's left and right hands. The third arm can hold an extra instrument while the fourth arm holds a camera.

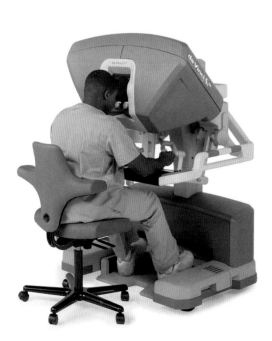

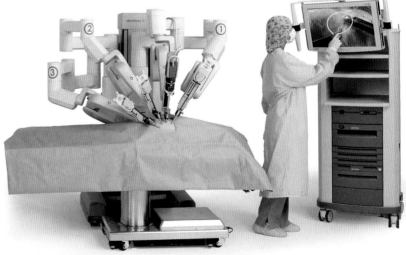

The da Vinci surgical robot is operated by a surgeon sitting at a console, while the robotic arms carry out the surgery.

Around 1,300 da Vinci robots are working in hospitals around the world. Nearly 1,000 of these are in the USA. Tens of thousands of operations have been carried out using them. Hospitals in developing countries cannot afford advanced technology such as surgical robots, so they are slipping further behind countries where high-tech medicine is practised.

WHAT'S NEXT?

Operating at a distance using a surgical robot is called telesurgery. In future, it could enable surgeons on Earth to operate on an astronaut in a space station. The further apart the surgeon and patient are, the longer it takes for radio signals to travel between them. With a surgeon in New York and a patient in France, the delay is 39 milliseconds (thousandths of a second) in each direction. Longer delays over greater distances make telesurgery impossible with current technology.

LINDBERGH

Surgeons and the robots they use to carry out operations don't have to be in the same room, or even the same city! In 2001, surgeons operated on a 68-year-old patient using a Zeus surgical robot. The surgeons were several thousand kilometres away in New York, USA, but the robot and patient were in Strasbourg, France. The operation was codenamed Lindbergh after the pilot, Charles Lindbergh, who made the first solo transatlantic aeroplane flight. This was the first time that major transatlantic surgery was performed by surgeons using robots. Since then, many operations have been performed in this way over long distances.

The da Vinci System translates a surgeon's hand movements into more precise movements of surgical instruments.

CHAPTER 6
humanoids

Very few of the robots in service today are built to look like real humans. Some scientists think that we will find it easier to deal with robots if they look like us. Robots that look like us will also be better able to move in and work with the buildings and machines that we have built for ourselves. Robots built to look like humans are called humanoids or androids.

Fitting in The artificial world that we work and live in – made up of furniture, buildings, vehicles etc. – is designed for people. Human-sized and human-shaped robots should fit into it better than other robots. Because of this, a lot of research is going on into the design and construction of humanoid robots. The most famous, most advanced and most successful humanoid robot is Honda's ASIMO.

ASIMO's joints move in the same way as human joints, but ASIMO has electric motors instead of muscles.

HOW IT WORKS

ASIMO sees the world through two cameras in its head. It hears the world through microphones. Its head, body and limbs are moved by 34 electric motors controlled by computer. They ensure that ASIMO remains perfectly balanced even when it is walking, running or climbing stairs. ASIMO can also find the answers to questions by accessing the Internet and then retrieving information such as news and weather reports.

ASIMO can walk, run and carry things in a very human-like way.

ASIMO The name ASIMO stands for Advanced Step in Innovative MObility. It looks like an astronaut wearing a backpack. There have been three generations of ASIMO, each one more advanced than the one before. The latest ASIMO is the result of 20 years of research. It can work automatically as a receptionist or guide, or deliver things.

ASIMO stands 1.3 metres high and weighs 54 kg. It can walk at a speed of 2.7 kph and run at 6 kph. ASIMO's battery pack gives it enough power to walk for up to an hour. The robot can recognise up to 10 faces and learn people's names. It understands some human gestures. When ASIMO sees

someone hold out a hand, it knows that the person wants to shake hands. When it sees someone waving, it understands and waves back. ASIMO can recognise stairs and knows how to climb them. It also knows its name and responds when it is spoken to by name. About 100 ASIMOs have been built.

FOR AND AGAINST

What are the advantages and disadvantages of using humanoid robots to do work?

For
- Humanoids are the best-shaped robots for working in a human environment.
- They can use normal products and tools designed for humans.
- They can do dirty and dangerous jobs that people don't want to do.

Against
- Humanoids are not (yet) as capable as humans in some respects, such as dealing with complex and rapidly changing situations.
- Robot parts wear out and break down, whereas humans are able to repair (heal) themselves when they suffer minor damage.
- Robots with Web connections could be infected by computer viruses that would interfere with their operation.

True to life Some robots look more lifelike than ASIMO, but they aren't as capable. Their designers have tried to make them look like real people. Their metal skeleton is covered with a lifelike plastic skin. These robots have hair, their eyes blink and their mouths move when they talk. Their hands and arms move in a lifelike way too. Some of these humanoids have been made to look like women. Robots like this are called gynoids. A very lifelike Japanese robot called Actroid-DER is one example of a gynoid. 'She' has appeared in television commercials and worked as a presenter at business events.

These lifelike humanoids don't have ASIMO's artificial intelligence. It has proved to be impossible so far to combine a very lifelike appearance with a high level of artificial intelligence. One way of doing this in future may be to move some of the intelligence from the robot to the Web. A robot with a wireless broadband connection to a powerful computer need not carry all of its information processing power and memory around with it. It might need to carry essential intelligence for basic activities like walking, balancing, avoiding obstacles and so on, but the rest of its knowledge could be stored elsewhere.

Intelligence tests Humanoids are being used to test theories about human intelligence. Scientists at Imperial

HRP-4C is a gynoid robot. It can move its lifelike face to make different expressions – anger (left), happiness (middle) and surprise (right).

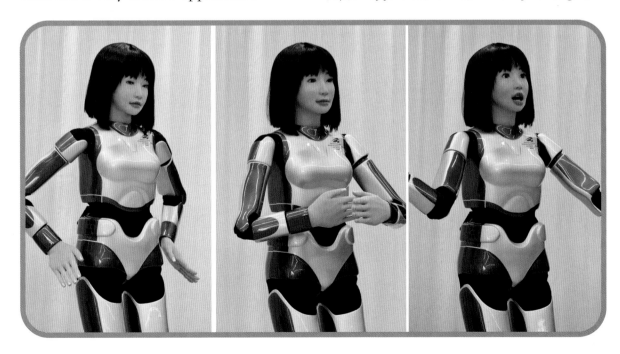

College, London, have created a model of a human brain in a computer. They will connect the brain to a humanoid called iCub, the size of a three-year-old child, to see if it behaves like a human child. They will watch how iCub learns about its surroundings, interacts with people and develops language skills. Working with iCub may help scientists to understand how humans learn and also help them to produce robots that learn and behave in a more natural, human-like way.

The iCub is a small, humanoid robot that is able to move, grasp objects and learn like a toddler. Scientists hope that the iCub will develop its capabilities and learn to interact in the same way as a child.

WHAT'S NEXT?

Teams of researchers in Europe, America and Japan are developing artificial skin for robots that can sense heat, cold and touch, like human skin. The robot skin is made of plastic or rubber with electronic sensors embedded in it. The skin is able to stretch and bend like real skin without damaging the sensors and circuits inside it. It may also be possible to heat the skin, so robot 'flesh' will feel warm, just like human flesh.

PATIENT ROBOTS

A humanoid robot is being used to help train dentists in Japan. It is taking the place of patients for trainee dentists to practise their skills on. This simulated patient is called Simroid. Its eyes blink like a real patient. Sensors in the robot's teeth turn on red lights if a drill goes too far. It even says 'Ouch' if the dentist is too heavy-handed!

Playing games One of the most difficult activities for a robot is playing a game like table tennis or football. The robot has to find and track a fast-moving object, the ball, move a hand or foot towards it quickly and then hit or kick the ball in the right direction. A lot of fast calculations are needed to get this right. And the robot has to keep its balance as it turns, runs and reaches for the ball. Some robot designers specialise in game-playing robots.

RoboCup Teams of robots from all over the world play against each other to win the Robot Soccer World Cup, or RoboCup. In 2009, approximately 400 teams from 35 countries competed. Like real football competitions, there are different leagues for different

A humanoid robot attempts to save a goal during the Robot Soccer World Cup or RoboCup championships.

The RoboCup project has set itself an ambitious aim. A league for humanoid robots was added to the competition in 2002. The aim is to develop a team of fully autonomous humanoid robots by the middle of the 21st century that can win a football match against a human team. It will not be any football team. It will be the winning team of the most recent World Cup.

robots. The robots are all autonomous. No-one controls them. If a robot falls over, it has to be able to get up by itself.

Competitive robot games are becoming increasingly popular and China held the first robot Olympics in June 2010. Only humanoid robots with two legs and two arms were allowed to take part in the games. Events included athletics and dancing.

Anyone for tennis? Tosy's TOPIO is a humanoid robot designed to play table-tennis as well as a professional player. By the time the ball hit by TOPIO's human opponent has travelled 20 cm, TOPIO has planned how to react. It uses four cameras to track the ball and two computers to calculate the ball's path through the air. TOPIO is clever enough to learn from each game and do better next time.

What's the point? Building robots that are at least as good as humans at playing games is great fun, but it has a more serious aim. A humanoid robot that can walk, run, balance, move to catch a fast-moving object and get up if it falls over would be a very capable robot for the home or workplace. Robot scientists and engineers are using game-playing to drive the development of more advanced general-purpose robots and artificial intelligence.

The table tennis-playing robot TOPIO 3.0 demonstrates its skills in 2009.

conclusion

More advanced robots are coming to our workplaces and homes. They will be intelligent enough to make their own decisions and adapt to changing circumstances. These robots will help us with housework and maybe look after us in our old age.

Good and bad In tomorrow's world, robots will probably become as commonplace as cars and computers are today. However, like every advance in technology, this will have advantages and disadvantages.

Human-sized robots will be powerful machines. How safe will they be? There have already been several cases of robots injuring and even killing people. The first death occurred in 1979 in the USA, when Michigan car plant worker Robert Williams was hit by a robot

FOR AND AGAINST

For
- Autonomous robots can make their own decisions.
- They are able to adapt to changes in their environment and circumstances.
- They can learn from their experiences.

Against
- Autonomous robots can sometimes make mistakes.
- They could take over the jobs of a lot of people.

arm. He was trying to take some parts out of a storage rack within reach of the arm when he was struck. Accidents have usually happened because a robot was not switched off before a worker crossed a safety barrier and came within its reach.

Tomorrow's must-have luxury could be a home-help robot. This robot carries a tray of food in a laboratory demonstration.

In your lifetime, you might be able to go for a drive in a taxi driven by a robot.

In future, much more advanced, fully autonomous robots may be working with us and perhaps sharing our homes. As long ago as 1942, the scientist and science-fiction writer Isaac Asimov invented three laws of robotics that every autonomous robot should follow in order to protect people and itself. Robots can be programmed with these rules, so that they don't do anything that endangers people. Some say that these laws should be updated now that robots are being used for military purposes.

Robots in society No-one knows if the general public will accept intelligent, human-like robots. For example, it is possible to build robot airliners that could fly themselves. They have not been built, because many people would not be willing to travel in an airliner without a pilot. New technology is not guaranteed to be popular, no matter how advanced it is.

ROBOT LAWS

The three laws of robotics written by Isaac Asimov are:

- **First law**: A robot may not injure a human being, or, through inaction, allow a human to come to harm.

- **Second law**: A robot must obey orders given to it by human beings, except where this would break the first law.

- **Third law**: A robot must protect itself as long as this does not break the first or second laws.

glossary

3D Three-dimensional. Having length, width and depth.

artificial intelligence The use of computer programs to give a robot human-like behaviour and decision-making abilities.

autonomous Able to control itself instead of having to be operated by a person.

defective Not functioning properly or faulty.

expendable Something that may be used up or that is easier to replace than to save or rescue.

fibre-optic cable A cable made of strands of glass, carrying information in the form of pulses of light.

gripper a tool fitted to the end of a robot's arm for grasping things.

gynoid A robot designed to look like a human female.

Hubble telescope A space telescope that was launched into orbit around the Earth in 1990 to obtain information about the universe.

humanoid A robot designed to look and act like a human being.

industrial robot A machine, often a computer-controlled arm, that can be programmed to work in a factory.

malfunction Failure to function or work properly.

mine An explosive device buried in the ground or put in the sea to destroy enemy troops, vehicles or ships.

mother-ship A large spacecraft or ship that controls, maintains or launches smaller craft.

nuclear powered operated by electricity generated from the heat produced by a radioactive fuel such as plutonium.

prototype The first example of something.

radar Radio detection and ranging. A method developed for locating aircraft and ships by sending out radio waves and receiving reflections from the craft.

radioactive Undergoing decay (changing from one element to another) by giving out particles or waves.

ROV A Remotely Operated Vehicle.

rover A vehicle used for travelling across the surface of a planet or moon.

service robot A robot designed to provide a service, such as carrying office supplies from place to place.

snakebot A robot designed and built in the shape of a snake.

solar panel a sheet of solar cells, which change light into electric current.

space probe An unmanned spacecraft carrying scientific instruments that is used to explore the solar system and send information back to Earth.

space shuttle A reusable spacecraft that carries humans and materials into space.

surface pressure The pressing effect of the atmosphere at the surface of a planet, caused by the weight of the atmosphere.

surveillance Constant watch kept over someone or something.

thruster A small rocket or gas jet fired to adjust the position or direction of a spacecraft, and also a propeller for steering a ship or underwater craft.

further information

Books

From Bugbots to Humanoids: Robotics by Laura Layton Strom, Children's Press, 2007.

Military Robots by Steve D White, Children's Press, 2007.

Rise of the Thinking Machine: The Science of Robots by Jennifer F VanVoorst, Compass Point Books, 2009.

Robot Explorers by Ron Miller, Twenty-First Century Books, 2007.

Robot World by Tony Hyland, Franklin Watts, 2009.

Robots by Clive Gifford, Carlton Books, 2008.

Space Robots by Steve Kortenkamp, Blazers, 2009.

Websites

Find out how robots work at this website.
http://science.howstuffworks.com/robot.htm

See for yourself what ASIMO can do.
http://world.honda.com/ASIMO

Read all about robot footballers.
http://www.robocup2009.org

Read about robot planes on Mars.
http://marsairplane.larc.nasa.gov

See what a robot astronaut looks like.
http://robonaut.jsc.nasa.gov

Learn more about the US Air Force's robot spy-plane, Global Hawk.
http://www.af.mil/information/factsheets/factsheet.asp?id=13225

Places to visit

The MIT Museum,
Cambridge, Massachusetts, USA
Display of objects of interest from Massachusetts Institute of Technology.
http://web.mit.edu/museum

Science Museum, London
Displays of all sorts of science and technology, including robot space probes.
http://www.sciencemuseum.org.uk

index